He turned around and saw two figures in the shadows running towards him with something in their hands. He started running himself, but it was clear that they were gaining on him. As he got to the end of the cobbled road, someone was waiting for him..

Dedicated to Marion, Angela, and my sister, Maggie, who encouraged me to write this book.

Me and my wife on our wedding day

The Backstreet Kid: The Laughter and Tears

By Doug Cowie

Part one

The laughter.

My story is based on my childhood memories of growing up in the 1960s in the backstreets of Hull and the people I met on the way who helped shape my life. It's a story of life, friendship and laughter. My story is based on real events and all places mentioned by me are real locations, although, sadly, many of these places have long gone.

It is not just my story, but our story, because it reflects the life of all of us, so if you too were born in the late forties or early fifties, I hope it will resurrect memories for you too. So as I go through those happy years, maybe it will take you back to your happy times and the people who changed your life.

I have taken the liberty of adding a lot of humour to my stories so that you might laugh with me.

All the names mentioned in my stories, with the exception of my own family, are fictitious so that I will offend no one but all the events took place as I relate them. As the sixties generation now approach old age, I think it's good to look back on how life was then. So I hope you will enjoy my story of a time now long gone but still alive in all of us.

I was born in the city of Kingston up on Hull (some like to call it Hull, but I like to be posh).

The street I was born in was called Trinity

street, just one of the many backstreets in Hull in the 1950s.

My mam was born in Hull, but my father was from the slums of Glasgow (not exactly Knightsbridge, is it).

Now my dad had a bit of a temper (well, to be honest, one hell of a temper, really). He was easily upset, not someone who you would want to get on the wrong side of.

Our house was very old and in a sad state of disrepair (if you ate too many beans, you'd blow the doors off, and to be honest, my dad liked eating beans).

Now we had no electricity upstairs in our house, so we had to make do with paraffin lamps (my dad got it on the cheap, if you know what I mean...).

We lived with my Grandad, and I was one of two kids at the time (more were to follow; I don't think my dad knew what "no" meant).

In the early fifties, my dad worked on a building site and he had a tendency to be a bit temperamental (ouch!)

One day my dad sat down on this bloke's seat in the work -cabin. Now this guy wasn't too happy about this and was a bit irate (oh dear! He didn't know my dad). He stuck his chin out and said to my dad, "Hey, Jock, you are sitting in my seat" (big mistake). Well, he didn't take to his tone of voice too well and hit him on the jaw (very temperamental, my dad, he wasn't known for his patience).

But the funny thing was when he came out of hospital (bless him), he became my dad's best mate (very wise). Now I know this is true because in the cold weather when they all sat in the work-cabin, this bloke would say to my dad, "Hey, Walt, come and have my seat by the stove where it's warm" (he was a very considerate man, this guy, although he would always stroke his jaw when he said it).

An unfortunate incident.

I was around one year old when I was a victim of a fire in our house. We were still living on Trinity Street at this time. This was to result in me being taken to the hospital with a badly burned arm.

Let me give you some details of this event.

My mam and dad had left me and my sister (who was a few years older than me) in the capable hands of my Grandad (now, this was not a good idea because he was inclined to nod off, bless him).

Well, my mam and dad had gone to the Lony (the local cinema). Meanwhile, I was by the open fire in my highchair, happily watching Grandad nodding off. Well the old sod fell asleep (I think he needed his sleep, bless him).

Unfortunately, my sister was playing with a bit of string near the open fire (she didn't have an Xbox, bless her, so she was a bit bored). Well, the string caught fire and as a result...

My armchair caught fire, too. Now, to be fair, my Grandad did apologize (while I was still smoldering).

Now when my mam and dad got back to the house, my dad wasn't very pleased because he'd decorated the kitchen (heart of gold, my dad, bless him).

Still, these things happen, and I did survive, and the fire was quickly put out.

Oh, by the way, I have just forgiven my sister after sixty-six years because I don't see any point in holding a grudge, because I'm a very forgiving person...

I love my sister. Really, she had a hard time with my dad. He expected so much of her, she often was the one who got the back of my dad's hand.

My mam had a tough time, too. She was the one who had to struggle to pay the bills.

Often there wasn't enough money to feed us all, so she depended on the kindness of the owner of the shop next door when she got things on tick (credit).

This is how life was for us all down on our street. There were no luxuries, only simple, basic necessities and plain, and often bland, food.

We were always hiding from the rent man. In them days, most mothers did not work but stayed home to look after their kids, so it was left to the men to earn the money. My dad worked in the building-trade and in them days, if you were laid off because of bad weather, you didn't get paid, so you can appreciate how difficult life could be for my mother.

We do a moonlight flit from Trinity Street.

We left Trinity Street in 1960 to more spacious accommodation in Middelton Street (it had a bigger bog, or if your posh, a bigger toilet).

To be honest, I think our previous neighbours were pleased to see us go. Well, let's put it this way: I heard they had a big street party after we left.

I know the landlord was pleased to see us go because he was always shaking when he came to my dad to ask him for the rent money (my dad didn't like it when people asked him for money, especially the rent man).

So, we moved to Middelton Street by doing moonlight flit, taking all our belongings with us on a handcart (well, it was 1960, we were skint).

Middelton Street was one step up from Trinity Street

(notice I said one step up, which means that it had one more step to the front door).

Settling into our new home.

So we had now moved into our new home on Middelton Street (otherwise known to us as bandit country).

Now when we moved there to our new house (or up market slum), there was my mam and dad, Grandad, my older sister (the one responsible for the fire down Trinity street), and my brother, our Rob, who was better looking than me (but only just). Well, there goes the neighborhood!

When we arrived at Middelton Street, we had very little furniture, so we sat on orange boxes and drank tea from jam jars (oh yes, we were very sophisticated in our house; only the best for us kids). We had a tatty table and an old tin bath that we all had a bath in (and if you were unfortunate enough to be last, the water was stone cold). When the tin bath was not in use, it was hung on a nail on the backyard wall. How we got beds, I don't know, but we had no bedding, so we had to make do with overcoats for blankets.

The first thing my dad did when we came into our house was to put a chemical bomb under the floorboards to kill the black-clocks (big black beetles).

Now in them days, we had no carpets, only lino, but for some unknown reason, we had a telly! (My dad always said you should get your priorities right.) How he got us a telly still remains a mystery to me to this day.

We had an open fire in the backroom with a fire guard in front of it (my dad was taking no chances with my pyromaniac sister, bless her).

I always remember my dad getting a good roaring fire going (I don't know why he didn't leave it to my sister, she's pretty good at getting fires going). My dad would get a good roaring fire going by putting newspaper in front of the fire to draw it, and often the paper caught fire (much to my sister's delight). He then quickly scrunched it up to stop it from burning.

In them days, we never had a proper breakfast, just a bit of toast done on the fire with some Stork margarine. My dad said, "it's better for you, son, it's less fat" (he was such a caring dad my dad...and a tight sod). We were just skint.

There were two rival gangs down our street; the "nutters" and the "crazies." We lived at 38, about halfway down between the "nutters" on one end of the street and the "crazies" at the other end of the street (this was not a good idea). However, we could always call on my dad for help (good idea) because they were all scared of my dad.

I remember we sometimes had neighbours complaining about us kids to my dad (the fools). I think they must have had a death wish because they never came back.

I remember on one occasion when they came to our house complaining about the noise (I think it was because we had all been eating beans the night before).

Well, this irate woman came to our house and said, "I'm going to get my husband to sort out your kids."

My dad replied, "Tell him to get his mates, he's going to need them" (very temperamental, my dad, he soon gets upset). Mind you, on the plus side, he was a bit of a healer; well, put it this way, he cured that irate woman's husband of constipation.

Arguments among neighbours was not uncommon down our street, but no one wanted to argue with my dad because of his quick temper.

Most arguments ended in name calling but were soon forgotten a few days later. We had a good relationship with most of our neighbours, and my dad and mam had some good friends down our street. Most people down our street helped each other, including my dad.

Life in the sixties was a life of change for us all. Who would have thought that with the advent of The Beatles and their music that attitudes to life and moral values would change forever? That decade would have a profound effect on my life.

Although I remember my childhood days from 1960 to 1963 quite well, it is the years that followed that are the most vivid for me. So I hope you will enjoy the rest of my story, too, as I continue to grow up.

Later in part two of my book, I will focus on just one year: 1967. This is a year that all people of my generation will remember so well, it was "The summer of love." This year gave birth to "The flower children" and a dream that would soon fade. We must have all been naïve to believe that we could change the world with music and free love. But it was a great time to be young, as many reading this book will testify to.

Still, 1967 will be a year that I will never forget because it was one of the happiest years of my life. It was the year I left school and the beginning of a new adventure for me and my mates. We all had so much fun growing up in the 1960s, and most people of that generation will tell you the same. My story is about life as I knew it.

I remember all the beautiful music of that time, The Beatles, The Stones, The Who. I also remember the great folk singers of the time like Dylan and Donovan, these were the singers that inspired me at the time with their protest songs against The Vietnam war and the fight for racial equality.

Anyway, let's now get back to my story...

A Time of change.

The year is now 1964, and it has been four years since we moved from Trinity Street.

I call this year the year of Vick, TCP, Pine disinfectant and Germoline (this was the first-aid kit my mam used in our house).

Although things had improved since we moved from Trinity Street, my mam still got things on tick (credit) at the corner shop and often didn't have enough money to pay the bill at the end of the week.

From 1960 to 1964, I went to the school at the bottom of our street, and it was here where I met my mates Razzar, Peter and Tony. However, I remember very little of the time I went to this school.

But I do remember the next school very well.

No one was in a hurry to go to Wilberforce High School, including me. I had been told about it's notorious reputation by ex-pupils, so you can appreciate I was in no hurry to get there....

Well, the time came for me to go to Wilberforce High School.

I can still remember my mam's words, "Dougie it's time to go to your new school."

Well, what did I do?! Well, I did what any sane person would do. I ran upstairs and locked my bedroom door with five padlocks and hoped that my dad couldn't get in (this was not a good idea).

However, my dad used a bit of psychology and said, "If you don't come down them stairs now, I'll kick your arse from here to land's end" (he had a way with words, my dad, bless him).

Well, I soon came to appreciate my dad's wise words and his eloquent use of the English language and decided to come downstairs.

So, I reluctantly got ready to go to school with my survival kit (just a few things, you know, like my stab-proof vest and a grenade).

Well, when I got there, it really wasn't that bad (apart from the two stabbings and four muggings, those teachers should really learn to deal with their anger issues).

When you went to Wilberforce High School you had to learn to live by your wits or your fists. I learnt to live by my wits...and two big mates (I didn't want to lose my good looks). Even the teachers were scary, they had names like Killer Kennedy (our science teacher).

I have decided not to mention any of the pupils' names because the SAS are still looking for them.

Oh, I'm only joking. They were not a bad bunch of lads really and they did teach me a lot about life like...robbery, extortion...

Mind you I consider myself really lucky; after all, I could have gone to a really bad school. To any of the lads reading this, it was a rough school, but I had some good mates and good times there. It made me appreciate my roots and working-class background.

Things you should know about my dad.

My dad liked his drink, particularly whisky, and often came home in an unpredictable state. Sometimes he was in a good mood after having a few drinks with his mates, other times he came home and didn't want to be sociable. In fact, he would easily be upset by even the smallest irritations, like for example, if my mam had done his dinner and it wasn't to his liking. He had a hell of a temper if someone got on the wrong side of him. And he was a real hard case; he wasn't frightened of anybody. He sometimes gambled his money and sometimes lost it all, and this added to his unpredictable nature. Often my mam had to ask for extra credit at our corner shop. These were hard times for my mam, although she often kept her worries to herself, not wanting to worry us kids.

But my dad loved us kids and taught us how to look after ourselves. He didn't take too kindly to anyone who upset us. I think my dad's temperament was the result of the hard times he had gone through as a kid in Glasgow tenements of the Grobals.

Our lives are molded by our parents, and my brothers and sisters are no exception. We all have my dad's temper, but we have learned to keep it under control.

Let me give you some more interesting facts about my dad.

I have already told you that my dad was a hard case (fact),

but here are some other things you should know about my dad. He had false teeth which made him look a bit like Red Rum when he smiled (which wasn't very often).

He also was a bit grumpy when he came home from work. I can remember him asking my mam to get him some dinner. So my mam brought him some egg and chips and gave it to him while he was sitting in his favorite chair (the chair was a bit like an explosion at a spring factory but it was still the must comfortable chair in the house).

Anyway, my mam brings in his egg and chips and gives it to him on his lap and he takes one look at it and says, “What the hell is this?” and then throws it over his head and it hits the back wall and then says get me something else (I thought to myself at the time, my mam’s cooking isn’t *that* bad). That’s one of my dad’s funny ways...

He could be quite unpredictable, my dad. However, he could be quite generous too. He frequently broke wind and would smile and say, “share that among yourselves.” (I thought to myself, that’s very gracious of you.) Another thing my dad would do was to soak his false teeth in bleach to get the stains out. (All these things I’m telling you are true, by the way.)

Once he was working on a building site and he stood on a nail and it went through his boot. He was off work for a few weeks (he really nailed that job...sorry, couldn’t resist telling that one).

My dad and his back problem (or, The Fiery-Jack incident)

Anyone who was living in the 1960s will remember a balm called Fiery-Jack. If you had a bad back or any muscular pain, you would rub Fiery-Jack on the painful area of your back and it would get very warm and ease the pain....

Well, my dad reached for the Fiery-Jack and rubbed it liberally on his back, but unfortunately, my dad wanted to go for a pee. However, my dad had forgotten to wash his hands. Now this was not a good idea because it wasn't only my dad's back that got very hot.

I can even remember the song on the radio at the time; its chorus went "goodness gracious great balls of fire!"

We had many laughs with my dad, too many to relate. This is just one incident that I remember so well. My dad had a funny side as well as a serious side and often had us kids in stitches, just by some of the things he did.

My mam had her funny side too. For example, when us kids had a bad chest, she would give us Vick. Now most mothers would rub Vick on their kids' chests, but my mam would also give it to us on a teaspoon with sugar on it.

I don't think she ever read the instructions on anything.

My dad and the Hoover man...

By the year 1965, things had begun to improve, although we still had very little by way of furniture.

Also, we still didn't have any carpets, only lino, but we did have a large mat in the backroom.

This brings me to an event that took place that I will always remember with laughter.

One day this guy came to our house trying to sell my dad a Hoover (big mistake, he didn't know my dad).

Well, this salesman was so enthusiastic and insistent about showing my dad how good it was (the fool).

So my dad let him in (well, the mat wanted a

good clean anyway, my dad thought).

Well this bloke started this contraption up and it made one hell of a noise and freaked out the cat!

At that, the cat ran through the door (pity it was closed at the time).

Well, the cat ended up with one hell of a headache and rather a contorted face...

I seem to remember that the cat had a bandage on its head for two weeks after that unfortunate incident.

Well, this salesman was smiling when he looked at my dad and said expectantly, "Well, what do you think? It's only..."

My dad turned to him and said, "Yeah, it's great, now bugger off" (it's never a good idea to ask my dad for money, he takes it personally).

Hey Walt, your front door on fire!!

Everyone likes fireworks except my dad.

Well, us kids wanted to buy some fireworks, but the problem was we had no money.

Well someone had to go to my dad and ask him for money, so I went to ask him because I was the bravest. To my surprise, he said yes!

Well, he went off to the shed to get a crowbar to open his wallet and give us a few bob to buy some sparklers (well, I did say a few bob).

Now my problem was I got a bit excited and lit mine while I was going out of the front door (this was not a good idea because the bloody net curtains caught fire).

Well I was now in a state of shock and quickly

ran out of the door, but I had forgotten to tell my dad that the front door was on fire.

Well, I ran down our road while the curtains were still alight.

Fortunately, a concerned neighbor knocked on our front-room window and shouted, "Hey, Walt, your front door on fire!"

Well, my dad moved so quickly he was given the nickname "Flash" after that (like someone had called him to the bar and told him there was a free pint there).

Fortunately, there wasn't much damage done, except the net curtains wouldn't need washing again.

Meanwhile, I desperately needed a change of underwear. Well my dad found me with my baklava on trying to look inconspicuous.

And you can guess what happened next.

I leave school and get a job.

I left school in 1967. The years I spent there had been a real education, but unfortunately not the education my dad expected.

Actually, I did learn a lot like forgery, robbery... (it's ok, I'm only joking again).

Anyway, I'm starting to digress from the next chapter of my story.

I started work as an apprentice electrician at a well-known dance hall, but the electrician decided to take early retirement for some reason when I started.

I didn't last long at that job... How was I to know that the red wire isn't earth?! Apparently, one of the punters found out and ended up with a crazy hairstyle...

Well, they decided then to give me a DJ job after the previous DJ went off work after suffering an electric shock. So they gave me his job, but I soon got sacked from that job. How was I to know that they didn't like Mozart?!

Anyway, I left there in 1969 (for some unknown reason they were pleased to see me go).

Now, I was out of work and my dad said to me, "You've got six weeks to get a job or I'm kicking you out."

(Very considerate man, my dad.)

So I quickly got a job. As it happened, I saw this job advertised in the employment exchange. It was a job working for the council on the roads (I thought that I could get my head down, zzzz). So I go for this interview with this manager from the council.

The interview went something like this: “Why do you want to work here?”

I said, “Because my dole money ran out.”

“Can you be serious for a minute?”

“Have you got a criminal record?”

“No, do I need one?”

He then said, “Do you have any qualifications?”

“What does that word mean?!”

He said sarcastically, “Are you in good health and sound mind?”

“Well, I’m healthy, but I won’t be for long if I don’t get this job.”

Feeling rather sympathetic, he said, “What do you mean?”

“Well, my dad said I’ve got to get a job or else he’s kicking me out.”

“Come on, it can’t be that bad.”

“You don’t know my dad, do you?”

Anyway, I got the job working on the roads.

So I started work on Big Jim's gang, who happened to be an ex-guardsman...I soon realized I wasn't going to get my head down.

Now the toilet facilities on Big Jim's gang left a lot to be desired. The toilet was just a small shed with a bucket and a toilet seat. So I said to Big Jim, "Hey Jim, there isn't a lock on this door."

He replied, "Don't worry, lad, we haven't had a lock on that door for five years and no one has stolen the bucket yet."

Well, while I was working there I decided to have a go on this five-ton road roller (this was not a good idea; I hadn't been on a five-ton roller before). I thought, it can't be that hard to drive. Well, I started this five-ton roller up but unfortunately, I didn't know how to stop the bloody thing.

Well there was chaos on the site, there were guys jumping over stacked curb stones six-foot high (I think some of them blokes could have been Olympic champions).

Well I got sacked again, and you know I'll always remember Big Jim's cutting words, "You're f— sacked!" Well, I now had to get another job again. Fortunately for my sake, I did.

Slasher Brown, the demon barber of Argile St.

I almost forgot to tell you about the demon barber of Hull—Slasher Brown.

In the sixties, all us lads wanted to have long hair like the Stones or The Beatles. But unfortunately, my dad had other ideas.

My dad used to say to me, “Son, you need a hair cut.”

I said, “But dad, my hair isn’t that long.”

He replied, “You need to have a decent hair cut like me.”

“But dad, you’re bald!”

“You’re going to have your hair cut, so no arguments.”

No matter how much I protested, I had to go.

Now this guy didn't have a clue how to cut your hair.

I think the last haircut he did was on Yul Brynner...

He said to this poor bloke he was giving a shave to, "I haven't seen you here for a while."

"No, I thought I'd wait until my scars healed up," he said.

I said to Slasher, "Can you give me a Tony Curtis?" He replied, "Who the hell is he? Does he live down Hawthorne Close?" (Need I say more?) When I got back to my school, they all had a good laugh and said, "Look who's been to Slasher" and "Have you thought of auditioning for the King and I?"

The Station Gang

In the sixties, me and my mates used to hang around one or two places, one of them places was The Station.

The Station was known for a notorious gang who terrorized young kids.

The Station gang were five hard cases who had the IQ of about twenty (I may have overstated their intelligence here).

They all looked up to their leader, Reg (not his real name), who was six foot six.

This moron's favorite pastime was grabbing hold of any unsuspecting kid and piercing his ear with a nail.

(Mind you, he was quite kind. It wasn't a rusty

nail, he didn't want them to get an infection.)

My mate told me that once Reg got caught nicking a bottle of milk off this pensioner and ended up in court. Apparently, the judge said, "I'm giving you six months." Reg sarcastically replied, "Six months? I can do that standing on my head." The judge replied, "In that case I'm giving you another six months until you get back on your feet again."

The trip to Glasgow

Every year my dad would take me and my brother Rob to see his brother Charlie in Glasgow.

We would go there in a Hull and Glasgow lorry.

He would bung his mate a few quid and he would take us all to Glasgow.

My dad used to say to us, "It's a bit of a holiday and it's better to see family rather than go to the seaside" (plus it saved him a few quid because he was skint).

It was a long never-ending journey, taking us hours to get there.

Well, when we eventually got there, we

stopped at our uncle Charlie's. Now uncle Charlie was a cross between the Kray twins and Al Capone.

He served his time in the navy on a ship, its name slips my memory now, but I think it might have been the Mary Rose...

Now, being young kids at the time, me and our Rob couldn't understand why Charlie had plenty of money and my dad was always skint.

Well, one day I was being curious and walked into Charlie's bedroom and opened one of the drawers of his dressing table and to my surprise I found a German Luger!!

Well, that night my dad and Charlie had a really good time drinking whiskey and singing. And even though they made one hell of a racket, none of the neighbours bothered complaining (I thought, how very considerate of them).

We never did tell my dad about the gun, I didn't think it worthwhile bothering him. And we never did go back to see uncle Charlie again... All this is a true story.

It's funny how you never forget certain things...

The youth club and St. Mike's Disco

In 1967, they built a youth club in the town center.

Its name I've forgotten now, but I do remember going there in my teenage years.

The idea was to get kids off the streets (that's a good idea).

The age of the kids was between 15 and 20 (not such a good idea). Now, the youth club had a woodwork room, a TV room and a stage where local groups would play.

Me and our Rob used to go to this club quite often, particularly to watch the groups who played there on a Saturday night.

If the groups were good, they let them live;

you don't want to know what happened to them if they were crap.

It wasn't long before things started to disappear (like the doors). They also closed the woodwork room because some prat had sawn the legs off the woodwork bench.

One night our kid (Rob) came home after being mugged at the youth club.

I was so angry (because he'd got blood on my shirt, now how thoughtless is that?!)

Well, I wasn't having some thug beating up our kid and ruining my best shirt.

So I went down to the youth club to sort out this guy, but when I got there, he was gone and so was the telly.

A night out at Saint Mike's Disco

St. Mike's Disco was situated in a well-known council estate (it had all mod cons like gaslights).

It was very popular with us lads because there were plenty of girls who went to that disco.

Now as you approached the entrance to St. Mike's, you had to run the gauntlet to get through the door. Now, there were a lot of lads asking for money to get in saying, "Give us a tanner" (that's six old pence in old money and was the entrance fee to get in).

If you were unfortunate to be the last to get through the doors, you had to pay for the rest of the kids to get in. I made sure I was the first, I didn't like parting with money (my dad taught me that, bless him).

When you got into the disco minus a few bob, if you were unlucky, then you would find it was quite dark apart from the UV lighting, which was great if you were wearing a white shirt (with no blood on it, of course). Now, the stage was well lit with psychedelic lighting, and there were girls dancing on the stage.

Now in them days the girls would dance around their handbags in their bare feet and the lads would be smoking fags. When they had finished smoking their fags they would then throw the cigarette butts while they were still alight on the floor; the girls soon started a new dance craze (I think it was called the hop).

I seem to remember there was a lad who was always off his face on drugs, and he was always standing on the girls' toes, and he was always getting punched. I think this unfortunate guy was given the nickname "The Panda."

I Learn to drive

About a year later, I was going out with this great girl. She said to me, "I want you to learn to drive so you can take me to the seaside." I replied, "I'm not really keen on learning to drive, it's going to cost me a lot of money." She said, "If you don't learn to drive, I will, and it will still cost you money anyway, because I know you would do anything for me."

"Ok, I'll learn to drive."

So I went to this driving school called The Last Chance driving school.

After I'd been driving for a while its name was changed to No Chance driving school.

When I started learning to drive at this driving school they had six cars; when I'd finished, they had three.

Now I had three driving instructors. The first one had a hart attack (he did recover, by the way, but only when I left). The second one had a nervous breakdown and the third was on Valium all the time he was teaching me.

Well I eventually did pass my driving test (I think they knew a good driver when they saw one). I will always remember that day. The sun was shining (my driving examiner was shaking), the roads were really quiet, not a soul on the road—I think there must have been some idiot on the road at the time.

Ok, I'll be honest, I wasn't that bad, and I did pass my driving test the second time. Although they were pleased to see me go. It did take a lot of patience to teach me, and I did cause some damage to one of their cars.

I must admit, though, that I'm still not keen on driving. I think it's because I keep getting these flashbacks (ha ha!).

A night out with the lads

It's seven o'clock in the evening, nearly time to leave the house. I've just had a strip wash and put on my Mod jacket (I love my Mod jacket, it's my prized possession). I can smell a strong odor of Vick that my mam had just rubbed on my youngest brother's chest. Meanwhile, I'm splashing on the Brut aftershave on my face (like you do when you want to impress the girls).

My dad comes in smoking a fag (he's so sophisticated, my dad), he's just been to the lavy (toilet). Well, it's either that or he's been through the motions.

I sort of knew he'd been to the lavy because my mam couldn't find the TV times (no luxury toilet paper then, I'm afraid, and you had to make sure you removed the staples).

Well, I keep splashing on this girl magnet when my dad comes in and says, “You smell like a bloody tart.” I reply, “It’s better than smelling of Lifebouy soap, anyway, if it’s good enough for Henry Cooper, it’s good enough for me”

(Henry Cooper was a famous boxer of the sixties who happened to be advertising Brut aftershave at the time).

I make my way to the front door looking really smart with my Mod jacket on and a new shirt, ready to impress the birds. As I step onto the front door step, the step that my mam scrubbed every day for years, I look forward to having a great night out with the lads.

I walked past the lamppost that had once been a gas lamp in the 1890s. The lamppost still had arms sticking out where once a piece of rope was tied and the kids used to swing from it.

I now walk to the top of our street where I pass on the way some Mods with their parkers on with their scooters, and I think to myself, how many mirrors do they need on them scooters anyway? Still, I give them a nod and say they look great (no sense in getting my head kicked in and getting blood on my new Mod jacket, is there?).

I now make my way to the Eagle pub on Spring Bank where my mates are waiting for me.

As I walk in I notice they all have a pint in their hands.

Razzar then opens his gob and says, "It's your turn to buy the next round, you tight bastard." I reply in the usual way, "I bought you one last night in the Botanic." Raz then says, "Yea, but we thought we was going to get us one each."

(So bloody ungrateful, my mates.)

So I said, "it's ok, lads, I'll buy you one each in the Botanic." All of a sudden, Razzar broke wind and Tony had an asthma attack (now I'm not saying they are related but...).

It was at this time that the bar suddenly became empty. It was then that Pete said, "I don't feel too good."

"Nor do I, it must have been them sprouts that Raz ate, the dirty sod. Let's go to the Botanic, even the beer in that place doesn't smell that bad."

Before I start part two of my book, I must tell you about us lads.

First, we all went to school together and we all stood up for each other just like brothers.

Razzar was a real hard case, not someone you would want to cross. But he always had girls falling at his feet (mainly because they were too weak to stand up). He was a well-built lad, with big hands and fists that could knock your head off if you were unfortunate enough to upset him. Only I could calm him down.

Tony was a real charmer and knew every chat-up line in the book. He was always smartly dressed like me.

Pete was a good-looking lad but a bit on the shy side. And then there was yours truly, both charming and cheeky. So watch out, girls, the boys are back in town.

We left the Eagle pub and went into the Botanic and had a few pints there and I bought the first pint (because I'm generous with my money, well I think so anyway). I remember at the time the song "Oh well" by Fleetwood Mac was playing. We then went on to the Locarno dance hall (known as Mecca by all who went there at that time).

It was here on that fateful night that I met my future wife. When I met this pretty girl, I had no idea how my life would change (I was always skint after that). I remember when we met she said, "I think we were meant to meet."

Now, Sue liked the simple things in life (like spending my money). I can remember meeting her dad, he said, "I'm so pleased she met you, she's costing us a bloody fortune."

I thought, great I'm going to be skint again...

I remember being at Mecca sitting on the balcony and she said to me, "I'd like to have two kids, a girl and a boy, what would you like?"

I said, "the bus home."

Her dad said, "How long do you plan on being engaged?" I replied, "How about ten years? Only I'd like to pay the mortgage off the bloody boots I bought her."

Anyway, we did get wed and we did have two kids and they did cost me a fortune like their mam but now they are both married and costing someone else a fortune. ....

Part two

...the tears

The story I'm about to tell is "a fictional story." And is set in the year 1967 in Hull.

And all events that take place are written as if they really happened. I have used real locations and names of streets and places I went to when I was a kid (with the exception of the following, The Sick Parrot, The Longwood Estate, and Whitewood Close). I have drawn on my own experience of how life was then when I was sixteen. All names are fictitious except my own family and myself, so I can give my story some emotional depth and a sense of realism.

Any resemblance to any person now living or dead is purely coincidental except for my own family.

The memories of a backstreet kid

Now let me begin to tell you about the events that were to change my life forever in the summer of 1967.

A description of Middelton Street in the 1960s

Middelton street had originally been built in 1890 and at that time it was apparently a desirable place to live. But in the 1960s, it was a very different place. The houses were infested with black-clocks (black beetles), cockroaches and mice.

Our house, like all the houses down our street, had no bathroom or running water upstairs.

Once a week we would all have a bath in a tin-bath in the backroom. When the tin-bath was not in use, it was hung on a nail on the backyard wall.

We had two coal fires, one in the kitchen where my mam did the cooking and one in the backroom. In winter, because we had no heating upstairs, we had no choice but to learn to live with the cold weather.

We had an outside toilet next to the coal house that we all had to use, and this often froze in the winter months.

We only had two bedrooms upstairs, a small one for us lads and a big one for my sisters. My mam and dad slept in the front room.

Us kids played on the bomb buildings, which were areas of waste ground that had once been houses.

This was the environment that we were all brought up in and we all learned to look after ourselves.

I looked at my hands. They were grazed with little drops of blood on the knuckles. I put my hand to my nose, which was now beginning to weep blood.

I now started to make my way home, knowing what response I was going to get from my dad, and it wasn't long before my expectations were confirmed.

As I opened the front door and made my way to the kitchen, I was greeted by a sneer from my dad. He said with a measure of contempt, "Did you win?" (My dad didn't like it if one of his lads lost a fight.) I responded by saying, "Does it look like I won?"

"I thought not, you will never be like your dad," he said with a laugh.

Party filled with anger and embarrassment, I said back, "Keep your nose out of my business."

"By the look of you, it looks like you should keep your nose out of other people's business." Then he laughed. "Oh, go to hell, dad!"

My mam said, "Come over here and I'll get some cold water for that bloody nose and some TCP for that grazed hand."

"Mam, stop bloody fussing, it's not broken, it's only a nose bleed. It will stop in a minute, I'll sort it out myself." So I went over to the cold tap and got a cloth, soaked it in water and held it to my nose.

"Well, what were you fighting about anyway?" my mam said. "That bloody girl across the road I expect," said my dad, laughing.

Looking down at my hand, which was now stinging from the TCP, I gritted my teeth and said, "He got a lucky punch, he won't get another chance" (and he didn't, much to my dad's delight).

I said to my mam, "I don't want anything to eat, I'll get a sausage roll from the corner shop." Then I said, "Oh, by the way, did you pay the bill? If you haven't, you won't get anything else on tick, mam."

"Yes, I paid it this morning, Doug, so you should be alright."

Turning to my dad, I said, "If you didn't go to the pub so often and gave my mam enough money, mam wouldn't have to run up such a big bill."

"Shut your bloody mouth before you lose some of your teeth to go with that bloody nose of yours."

"That's your answer to everything dad in it." Then I left the kitchen to get ready to go out.

I poured some warm water in a bowl and took a flannel and some Lifebouy soap and had a strip down wash. I thought to myself while I was getting washed that I wish mam would get some decent soap rather than this rubbish. Then I took a towel and dried myself and splashed plenty of Brut on myself to mask the smell of soap. While I was doing this, I said, "good old Henry."

Then I made my way over to Toney's house at the top of our street and to my surprise he was ready, for once (I never knew what took him so long). He was always late, he was like some tart getting ready to meet her boyfriend. I said to him, "We're going to Peason's Park." This was our regular meeting place when we were skint.

"Has your dad got a job yet, Tony?"

"No, mam said he needs to get off his fat arse and get a job."

"What was his last job, Tony? A chariot builder?" I said with a grin.

"Very funny," Tony said with a scowl.

"And what about that brother of yours? Is he still going out with that redhead?"

"Yeah, I think so."

"Why doesn't he go out with a bird with some hair?" He didn't think that was funny either. "Is Razzar meeting us at the park?" I asked.

"No, he's got a part-time job now."

(Then I thought to myself, I bet some of Ronny's Gang will be there, and I haven't brought a change of underwear.)

The notorious Ronny's Gang sometimes went to the park, and it wasn't to do any bloody gardening.

After leaving Tony's house we made our way to the bottom of our street and turned left at the school, then walked down the ten-foot (an alleyway) to the road that led to the park to find some fit birds.

A description of Peason's Park

Peason's Park was only around ten minutes' walk from Middelton Street. It was well kept and looked after by the

park authorities. It had originally been called Peoples Park, but the name was later changed to Peason's Park.

It covers an area of 20 acres. If you approached it from Park Road, as we did when we were kids, and followed the path, you would come to the children's playground that now is enclosed by a high fence.

But if you turned left past the lake, you would then come to a white brick building that resembled a bus shelter. This shelter was affectionately known to us kids as the cow shed.

This building was in front of a big Victorian conservatory. (The cow shed was a favorite place for courting couples because of its discreet location.) The cow shed is no longer there now, but was demolished years ago because of drug issues, so I've been told.

I meet San for the first time

We were now close to the park when I turned to Tony and said, "I miss Razzar, you can always depend on him when you need him."

"Yeah, he's not scared of anybody, Raz, except your dad."

I smiled, "Everyone scared of my dad."

"What job is Raz doing then?"

"I think he's doing some work for a builder somewhere."

I turned to Tony and wrinkled my nose. "Have you noticed Razzar pongs a bit?"

"Are you going to tell him?"

"No, I'll give that a miss, he's not one for taking hygiene advice."

"Mind you I did hear that he went to the chemist, asked for some deodorant and this guy behind the counter said, 'Certainly sir, ball or aerosol?' Raz looked at him and snarled and then said, 'Are you being bloody funny or what? I want it for my armpits, ok?'" We both laughed and said, "That's Razzar, not too bright."

The park was very popular with the lads and girls in the early evening when the mothers had taken their brats home. And it was now six o'clock, but for some reason it was eerily quiet for this time of day.

I said to Tony, "Are you thinking what I'm thinking?"

"Yeah, it looks like Ronny and his gang might be here.

Although, I can't see any sign of him or his gang."

"I think we'd better be ready to leg it if we see them," I said, being a bit apprehensive.

Then, to our surprise and delight, we saw a couple of tasty birds walking towards us and I forgot any fear I had. One of the girls was a bit taller than me, she had auburn hair, beautiful blue eyes and pouting lips, and she was blessed with a lovely figure. I was smitten straight away.

Tony's girl was a little shorter with jet black long hair and very pretty with brown eyes. We all hit it off straight away and made our way to the cow shed.

"What's your names, girls?" I said. The girl who I was smitten with answered, "My name is Casandra, but don't call me that, just call me San."

"And my name is Sally, but just call me Sal," Sally butted in.

"Well girls, it's your lucky night, you've just met two great lads."

"And modest and cheeky too, by the looks of it," said San with a smile. We then reached the cow shed and we all sat down.

"I noticed, San, you have a bit of a different accent to us lads. Where are you from?"

"Hull, the same as you two, but my dad was from Stockport."

"You said came!"

"Yeah, my dad's in hiding, well that's what he told my mam in his letter."

I laughed. "I thought I was the only the comedian here, I've heard that they don't bury the dead in Stockport but just stand them up in bus shelters with a woodbine in their gob and a pint in their hand."

San said, "I've heard that one before."

"Not the way I tell it, San."

"What's your names?"

"Oh sorry, I'm forgetting my manners, my name's Doug and this is my mate, Tony."

"Where do you girls live?" said Tony. "The Orchard Park Estate," said San. "Oh dear. Isn't that called bandit country?" I said. San laughed, "Oh come on, it's not that bad, where do you lads come from?"

"Middleton street on Spring Bank," I replied. "And you have the cheek to call Orchard Park bandit country," said San. "Anyway, we come from the posh area," said Sally with her nose in the air. Then we all laughed.

Tony and Sal then went off somewhere private leaving me and San alone.

We were now alone together so I reached over and looking into her beautiful blue eyes and gave her a kiss.

We spent some time together talking about where we lived and our parents. Then I said, holding my breath and desperately hoping the answer would be yes, "Can I see you again?"

She gave me a warm smile, "Do you want to?"

Looking again into her blue eyes, I said, "Yes, I do."

"Where shall we meet then?"

"Let's meet on Friday at our local pub."

"But we'll all get kicked out, we're all

underage."

"Not where we go, I'll give you my number."

"You've got a phone! How can your dad afford a phone?"

"It's a perk of the job so they can call him when they need him."

San then gave me a passionate kiss that I still remember to this day. San looked me in the eye, "We have to go now, we're meeting some friends, but I will give you a ring from the phone box." It was then when Tony and Sally came back.

And the girls then went off to meet their friends.

Not long after the girls had gone, we heard familiar voices in the distance. And they saw us. "Run! It's Ronny and his mates!" I shouted, "If they catch us, they will kick our heads in." We then ran for our lives, but they were not far behind and they didn't look that pleased to see us. By some miracle we managed to get far enough away. Then I shouted out, "Did your mam ever find out who your dad was?"

Ronny then shook his fist and shouted back, "I'll have you soon, you bastard."

After narrowly missing having our heads kicked in by Ronny and his gang, we made our way home back to Middelton Street.

On our way home, Tony turned to me and said, "Why don't you get your dad to sort out Ronny?"

"What! And give my dad the satisfaction of calling me a coward? Anyway, I'm not scared of that nasty aggressive bastard, terrified, yes, but not frightened."

"But you sorted out that kid down our street."

"Yeah, but he wasn't built like the incredible hulk."

It was now getting dark and I was getting really hungry. That sausage roll wasn't very filling. So, I was willing to risk my mam's cooking.

When I got in, my dad wasn't there, he was working a late shift. My mam said, "Just in time, Douggie. I have just made meat and tatie pie, any later and I would have given it to the cat."

"Don't do that, mam, we can't afford the vet's bill." I then laughed. However, my mam wasn't amused nor was the cat (after all, he'd had a narrow escape).

He then looked at me with a smile on his face as if to say revenge is sweet.

I didn't stop up late that night but decided to have an early night.

When I got up in the morning, my brother Rob was eating some toast (I hated my brother, he was better looking than me). I also had two sisters; one very young and another older than me.

I often felt sorry for my older sister because my dad was so strict with her; when my older sister went out, she had to be in at eleven o'clock at night, any later and she was in big trouble.

My dad always insisted on meeting my sister's boyfriends. If he liked them, he let them live. If he didn't, they went out horizontal. Even if he did like them and they left the house standing, they were still on Valium for the rest of their lives. But me and our kid Rob could do whatever we liked (very fair man, my dad, bless him).

My mam was a lovely and kind woman and had to put up with a lot from my dad, but that's another story. My dad as I've already said was a hard man, but being brought up in the Gorbals in Glasgow, I suppose he had to be. In spite of this, he loved us kids.

My younger brother Reg was the quiet one until someone upset him, then he could be nasty sod like my dad.

Well, I asked our Rob for a couple of quid so I could take San to the pub and told him I'd give it back to him next Friday when I got paid.

All I had to do now was wait for Friday night to come.

I meet Razzar's girlfriend for the first time.

Although I had to borrow a couple of quid from Rob, I still had enough to meet Razzar and Tony in the pub on Monday night. San had phoned me to say that she and Sally would meet us on Friday evening. It would be a long wait, but it would be worth it. So with a couple of quid in my pocket, I made my way down to the pub.

To my surprise, Razzar was there with his girlfriend.

Now I must tell you about Raz's girlfriend Betty. Betty was a rather big girl, when she sits down, she needs two bar stools. It was once said, when she was running away from three coppers, that she broke wind and she blew their helmets off. She has more chins than a Chinese phone directory. I'm only joking, she was a big girl but still attractive.

Razzar introduced me to Betty. "This is my babe, isn't she cute? I met her at the chippy at the top of our road. She was battering this fish at the time."

I thought to myself, Yeah, and I bet it didn't survive. I shook her hand and just managed to get my fingers back.

"Hi Betty. I'm pleased to meet you. My name is Doug, I'm the generous one."

Tony and Raz roared with laughter and Tony said, "Doug's got short arms and deep pockets."

I tried to look hurt and then smiled, "Tony, you've hurt my feelings now, I'll prove to you that's not true and get the next round in." So I went to the bar and bought four pints. (Betty thought she'd start on the shorts first). I then came back to a table full of pint glasses, and Betty made space for four more.

I said to Razzar, "Tony's told me you've got a part-time job."

Raz replied, "I got sacked."

"What for?!"

"For being late."

"That's a bit unfair, Raz, how late was you?"

"Two days"

"Two days?!"

"Yeah, I wasn't feeling too good, I think I ate a dodgy curry."

"Sorry to hear that, Raz."

I turned to Betty and said, "How are you, Betty?"

"Alright," she said apathetically.

"What's up, Betty?" I said, trying to be sympathetic.

"It's her dad, he's started his new job," said Razzar.

"And he hates it," Betty replied.

"Why doesn't he just pack it in and get another job?"

"I asked him that, but he said he needs to get his head down."

Betty's dad wasn't known for his work ethic. I think his last job was school prefect.

I took a sip of my pint and wrinkled my nose in disgust, "The beer here doesn't get any better, does it?"

"I know it's crap isn't it," said Tony. "I went to Eddie (the landlord) and complained and all he said was, 'It's ok for you, you've only got four pints, but I've got three barrels of this rubbish and I've got to get rid of it, and because you lot are underage I thought I'd give it to you lot."

'Oh, thanks,' I said. And his reply was, 'Well, if you lot don't like it you can...off somewhere else.'"

"Well, at least we can get a seat here," I said.

Razzar then changed the subject. "I hear from Tony that you both had a bit of bother last night from Ronny and his gang." Raz's eyes narrowed and a twisted smile appeared on his face.

It was clear that Razzar had met Ronny somewhere before.

"Me and Ronny have got unfinished business."

"You've met him before, Raz."

"Yeah, I've met him before, and I've got a feeling that we will be meeting again very soon." Razzar's face was full of malice. He wouldn't say anymore but just drained his glass.

We talked for a while about other things and then I noticed that Pete wasn't there. "Where is Pete?"

"He's got a new girlfriend, so I doubt you'll see him for a while," said Razzar. Raz then turned to Betty and said, "But she's not as pretty as my babe." I didn't say a word but just smiled in agreement. Then I looked at my watch and said, "I've got to be going now, lads, I've got to be at work early tomorrow."

"Oh, I forgot to tell you, Raz, me and Tony won't be here on Friday, we've got a date with two tasty birds."

"I know Doug, Tony told us, have a good time and behave yourselves."

"Why, of course, Raz, I always do," I said with a grin.

Mam, why do you put up with this?!

I woke up early and made my way downstairs, having no stair carpet, each step creaked under my feet, but it didn't wake up my brothers or sisters. I went straight to the lavy then came in and washed my hands in the kitchen sink. I then went to the pantry and got some bread to make myself some toast. Having got a fork, I was toasting the bread in front of the fire. Dad had already gone to work. My mam had just come in with a cup of tea.

It was then that I noticed my mam had been crying.

"What's a matter, mam? How did you get that black eye ! Did my dad do this?"

"He didn't mean it, he was sorry afterwards."

I put my arm around my mam's shoulder and gave her a hug. I was full of anger and upset that my dad would do this to her. Gritting my teeth, I said to mam, "I'll have a word with dad when I get to work and tell if him if he ever touches you..."

"NO! leave it."

"But mam, he needs telling."

"Doug, it's not often this happens, it's just your dad's having money problems at the moment."

"That's no bloody excuse, he's still got money to go to the pub, or is he gambling his money away again?"

"No, he's stopped gambling now, it's not that."

"What is it then?"

"We've still got a lot of debt on at the moment and struggling to keep on top of it."

"Mam, do you want me to start giving you a few more quid each week?"

"No, Doug, you are already giving us more than you should, and Irean (my older sister) starts her new job next week so that should make a big difference."

"Are you sure, mam?"

"Yes, I'm sure, don't worry."

"I'm still going to have a word with dad."

"NO! Please leave it, you will only make things worse."

"But he needs telling, mam."

"No, son, I'm sure everything will be sorted out soon, and I don't think it will happen again."

"If it happens again, mam, I'll take the hammer to him and sort him out."

"Don't ever say that again! He's still your dad, now just get yourself ready for work."

So, I did as my mam wanted and kept my mouth shut and got ready to go to work.

My dad never hit my mam again after that.

Friday night, a night out with the girls.

Friday night eventually came, and I went through the usual ritual of getting ready. I had a strip-down wash but this time I'd bought some decent soap (I'd had enough of using Lifebouy soap).

We had arranged to meet the girls at 7 o'clock outside a department store called Hammonds near the bus station. Before I left the house, I made sure I paid back the money I owed my brother and then I went to Tony's house.

Me and Tony then walked into town. It was only a ten-minute walk to the town center from our house, and we arrived a few minutes before the girls.

When the girls came, they looked great. San was dressed in a purple dress that complimented her lovely figure, her makeup had been skillfully and carefully applied, and she looked beautiful. Her perfume filled my senses and drew my attention to her eyes. I gave her a passionate kiss and then she responded by giving me another.

Sally too had made an effort to impress Tony with her black dress and long black hair.

"Well this place better be good after all the effort we girls have made to get ready," said San.

"Only the best for you girls," I replied.

Tony gave me a look as if to say, I'm not convinced.

"I thought we'd all go and have a burger first."

We all then walked to the Timer-Burger (a bit like McDonald's but cheaper, well, a burger's a burger, no sense paying through the nose, is there).

When we got there and sat down, San said with a laugh, "Well you two certainly know how to spoil us girls, don't you?" I said back with a cheeky smile, "I know, I'm a victim of my own generosity."

"More like you are both a couple of tight bastards," said Sally.

"Now don't forget, girls, we are taking you both to a classy pub afterwards."

"And what's that, Doug? The Dogs Bollocks?"

"Now San, you're hurting my feelings, and besides that, the seats there aren't that comfortable."

"That's what I like about you, Doug, you are so considerate."

"Well I do try, San."

"Well, what's this pub called, Doug?"

"The Sick Parrot."

"The Sick Parrot?!" said Sally.

"It's quite a nice pub, really, Sally, it serves some classy cocktails," and then he turned away and smiled.

"Classy to you, Doug, means it's got carpets and toilets."

"Yes, and clearly marked male and female, San."

"Well, I suppose we won't all get thrown out for being underage there."

"I can assure you of that, San."

"That's only because their chucking people in," said Sally.

San then turned to Sally and said, "Come on, Sal, let's give it a try."

When we got to The Sick Parrot we got a lovely seat there and sat down (away from the broken glass and empty bottles).

We were having a great time drinking and laughing when Tony mentioned Ronny and his gang. Well, everything went quiet in the pub, you could hear a pin drop.

San's face turned pale, "What did you just say? Did you say Ronny and his gang! why didn't you mention him before? That guy is a real nasty bit of work."

"You've heard of him before?"

"Who hasn't heard of him?" said Sally in horror.

"Please keep well away from him, Ronny is real nutter, not a bloke you mess with."

At this point I decided to tell a few jokes to change the mood, but I was soon to find out how right they were.

After we left the pub we all walked down to the bus station and escorted the girls on to the bus. We then kissed them goodbye and arranged to meet them the following evening at Queens Gardens.

A description of Queens Gardens

Queens Gardens had once been the Queen Dock before it was partly filled in in 1930. It was then turned into beautiful gardens for the public.

In the early sixties it had been one of the favorite places for me and my mates to go to play. The Gardens are enclosed by a wall with eight entrances, two at each end. It now has an avenue of trees down its center and is very pretty in the summer. At the bottom of the gardens is a

Technical College, and in front of the college is a massive monument to William Wilberforce, a leading anti-slave campaigner in the eighteenth century. It was in front of this monument where I would wait for my future wife three years later.

An Evening with the girls in Queens Gardens

It was a beautiful summer's evening when me and Tony arrived at The Queens Gardens.

I had always loved this place since we were kids. We spent many happy hours playing by the fountain here by the lake, soaking each other to the skin. And then laughing our heads off.

And here we were, years later me and Tony dressed up in our best gear, waiting for our girlfriends.

It didn't take long for the girls to arrive, and they both looked real babes. As San approached me I felt my heart beating faster, and when she kissed me I felt like I was walking on air.

We found a bench and all sat down, then started to chat.

San asked me, "Do you have any qualifications?"

"I've got a survival certificate."

"What, in swimming like?" (She was such an eloquent speaker).

"No, just survival. What about you, San? Did you get any GCSEs?"

"No, not any."

"That means we both have a lot in common then."

"What do you mean, Doug?"

"Well, we're both thick then."

"Don't be so bloody cheeky." I then laughed.

Tony (big mouth) then said, "Do you remember when the geography teacher asked you where the English Channel was and you said, "I don't know, Miss, we can't get that channel on our telly."

San then laughed and so did Sally, so I replied, "Anybody can make a mistake, anyway, what about you, Tony and the RE teacher?"

"What do you mean?"

"Well, Mr. Blackwood asked you who knocked down the walls of Jericho and you said, 'It wasn't me, Sir! I think it was that kid from

4B2.'"

Tony's girlfriend laughed, then Tony said, "Anyway, Miss Greenwood had a crush on me."

I laughed, "How do you make that out? You were rubbish at maths."

"Well, she always put little kisses next to my sums."

The girls both laughed, and San said, "You're not right in the head, you two."

"We are just two backstreet kids with crap chat-up lines, San."

We were all having such a good time when we were approached by three lads who thought they were hard cases.

The biggest looked at me, then Tony, then said, "What are you doing with these two wasters? Why don't you two come with us?"

I clenched my fists and gritted my teeth, then I said,

"If you lot know what's good for you, you'll get running now."

"Who's gonna make us?"

Stepping forward I said, "I will."

San then said to me, "Leave it, Doug," and then looked at the lads and said, "Just go before someone gets hurt."

The big lad then replied, "Like who?"

I then stepped up to him face to face, "Like you." The others now legged it, leaving me and him facing each other. Someone now had to step down and it wasn't going to be me. Then he backed off from the confrontation and started walking away. After walking a few yards, he then turned around and said, "You don't know who I am, do you?" I was just about to go after him when San held me back. "He's not worth it, let him go."

Tony then said, "What do you think he meant by that, Doug?"

"I don't know, Tony, and I don't really care, let's just go to the Sick Parrot." As I was walking down with San, she turned to me and said, "Were you scared there?"

"Everyone gets scared now and then, San, but it's about learning to control that fear, my dad taught me that."

The following day when I'd finished work, I was walking back home from work down Spring Bank. I was not far from home when I bumped into the same lad coming out of The White Rose fish shop near Middelton street.

He stepped up to me, "That girl of yours is a bit of alright, the only problem is she's with the wrong lad. You should hand her over to me." He then threw a right hook at me but he was too slow. I ducked and came up with a right punch to his stomach. He moaned as he fell to the ground. “Stay down! Or you will really get hurt.” He didn’t take my advice, but got to his feet and threw another punch, only this time I hit him first in the mouth. He then spat out a tooth and said, still holding his tooth in his hand, “You made a big mistake, now I’ll tell you who I am. I’m Ronny’s brother, and you’ll pay for this.”

“Go running to your big brother. I don’t care, and book yourself into a good dentist while you’re at it. He then walked off alone, his mates had already deserted him.

I thought it wise not to tell San. I didn’t want to worry her, but I told Raz, he just said, “He got what he deserved but from now on watch your back, Ronny will come for you.”

Some good news, Ronny been locked up.

Me and San spent more time together now, sometimes it was at her house, sometimes she came to me. Other times we went to The Queens Gardens or to the pictures.

Tony and Sally had broken up and were now going their separate ways. Tony was never one for long-term relationships.

When we went to her house, her mother kept an eagle eye on us. Whenever me and San were in her backroom her mam would say, "Tell him to keep his hands to himself. I don't want you getting pregnant." It was her way of saying be careful (not that her mum need worry. San was an old-fashioned girl and believed in moral standards). Yet we were so much in love...

1967 was a beautiful summer, and I remember it so well for so many reasons...

I can still remember one Sunday afternoon coming out of my house and walking down our street in the warm sunshine, just watching the kids playing.

I remember seeing this cute little girl with a mucky face shuffling along in her mam's shoes, pushing her toy pram. As I continued down Middelton street, I passed the bomb buildings, and on there I saw three kids playing with dustbin lids and crudely made wooden swords. Just like I did some years before. Then I saw some young lads playing marbles. Looking back, it all seems like a dream now.

When I got back to my house, my mam said, "Tony's on the phone."

"I'm coming, mam."

"Hi Tony, how's it going?"

"Doug, I've got some great news."

"What's that, Tony?"

"It's Ronny."

"What about Ronny?"

"Guess what? They've locked the nutter up."

"Are you serious! Ronny's under lock and key!"

"Yeah, that bastard, apparently he was caught nicking fags from the local shop."

I breathed a sigh of relief and then said, "At last we are out of the brown stuff. That's great news, Tony, we will have to have a drink to celebrate."

"Yeah, Doug, but it's your round."

"But I got the last one in, Tony."

We both laughed.

However, it wasn't going to be that simple, he would soon be out, and he would be coming for me...

San comes to my house.

San arrived at the usual time and knocked on our door. My dad got there first and said, "Oh it's you. Doug, San's at the door."

"Do you have to be so ignorant?" He just walked away, unconcerned.

"Is everything ok?"

"Yeah, just ignore my dad, he's skint again and grumpy."

"Come into the backroom."

"Ok, but no funny business, alright? I'm a good girl."

"As if, San," and I gave her a cheeky smile.

And she was a good girl, too, much to my frustration.

"Hey! San, I've got some good news for you."

"And what's that, Doug? Are you going to spend a few bob?"

"What do you mean, San? I'm just careful with my money."

"No Doug, you're just a tight sod."

"Oh San, you can be so cutting sometimes in the things you say, and you know how sensitive I am," then I smiled.

"Ok Doug, what's this good news?"

"Sit down on the settee and I'll tell you."

So San sat down and eyed me suspiciously.

"It's Ronny, he's been locked up."

San's face lit up and she gave me a long passionate kiss.

"That's great news, even better than you spending a few bob, because you do know he's gunning for you, don't you?"

"Who told you that?"

"A friend of mine knows one of his gang and he said Ronny's pretty pissed off with you."

I felt a chill down my spine for a moment, then said, "Don't worry, he's locked up now, let's change the subject. Let me tell you this joke."

San looked up at me and rolled her eyes, "If you must."

"Did you hear about the blind man who went skydiving?"

"No."

"It scared the hell out of his dog."

San laughed, "That's quite funny for you, Doug."

She then put her hands around my neck and gave me a kiss. She then looked me in the eye and said, "If you ever hurt me, Doug, I will never forgive you."

"San, I will never break your heart because it would break mine too if I did."

She then said to me, "Why can't you say them three words to me?"

"It's not my style, San, anyway you know I do."

"I wish you would say it now and then because I love you with all my heart...

A tragic accident...

Pete gave Anna a kiss and then got on his motorbike.

Anna said, “Pete, take care on that bike, no speeding, ok?”

“Anna, don’t go on so, you know that I can handle my bike. I’ve been on my bike hundreds of times.”

“I know, Pete, but for some reason I feel really uneasy today.”

“Anna, how many times have you said that to me? You’re just being daft.”

Pete kickstarted his bike, then turned to Anna, “You know, Anna, you might be daft sometimes, but I do love you. Anna came over to him and gave him and a kiss, "just be careful, alright?"

Then Pete rode off on his bike without a care in the world.

The road conditions were ideal for riding his bike, the sun was shining and there wasn't a lot of traffic on the road. So he speeded up and enjoyed the thrill and exhilaration of being free.

He was only about a mile from home when he stopped at the traffic lights and prepared to turn left. It was just then when an articulated lorry pulled up beside him. Then just as the lights turned onto green and Pete was about to turn left down the road that led to Pete's house, the lorry turned too, but he hadn't seen Pete on his motorbike. Pete was caught under the wheels of the lorry and killed instantly.

Doug, I have some bad news, Pete's been killed.

Everything had been going so well, Ronny was in prison, and me and San were so happy together...

But our lives were soon to be shattered by one phone call, and it was only the start of a series of events that would change my life forever.

It all began one sunny day in late August. I was waiting for San to come down to my house when the phone rang. My mam picked up the phone and within a minute she passed the phone onto me, "It's Tony, he asked to talk to you, he sounds really upset." I took the phone off my mam wondering what had happened to upset him. "It's Doug, is everything alright?"

For a minute Tony didn't answer. "Tony, can you hear me?"

"It's Pete, Doug."

"What about Pete? Is everything alright?"

"Pete's dead, Doug, he's been killed." Then Tony began to sob.

"What...what...do you mean, he can't be... what's happened?" I was struggling to get my words out.

"Pete was killed yesterday on his way home in a traffic accident by a truck."

"How do you know?"

"His brother came over to my house this afternoon and told me. His mam and dad are in a right state and Anna is in a state of shock and can't speak, they only got engaged last week, it's heartbreaking."

I was struggling to get my head around what Tony had just said, already my eyes were filling up. My mam put her arm around my shoulder and said, "What's a matter?"

"It's Pete, mam, he's been killed."

My mam didn't know what to say but just put her arm around my shoulder. "I'm so sorry, Doug, you were such good friends."

"Tony, does Razzar know?"

"Yes, I've told him, he's devastated. Betty's

with him now."

"Thanks, Tony, I'll tell San."

San arrived a few minutes later and after I told her she wept with me.

Pete's funeral was the following week, and we were all there. We all wept together at the service. Anna was inconsolable, and his mam and dad were in a terrible state. Pete's brother was doing his best to keep everything together. I have never seen Raz cry. He was such a hard case, but that day he wept like a kid who had lost his mum. Betty put her arm on Razzar's shoulder like a mam comforting her son in a time of distress. Tony too didn't hold back the tears. We had been brothers, and now one of us was gone forever.

We all met together at the Botanic. San was there, too, giving me her emotional support. We talked of the good times we had together at school and in Peason's Park. When we had finished talking of the good times we had, we left the pub very sad, but all of us agreed we must get on with our lives.

A few weeks later we all met together under happier circumstances to celebrate Razzar and Betty's engagement. Razzar and Betty had got engaged! Who would have thought that? I reckon Betty must have had Raz in a headlock, after all, she had bigger muscles than Razzar.

My mam wants me to pack you in!

Around a couple of weeks later, San came to me in tears.

"What's a matter, San? Who's upset you? I'll knock seven bells out of them."

"It's my mam, she wants me to pack you in."

"Oh dear! I think I'd better get Raz, she's bigger than me."

"It's not funny, Doug, I think she means it."

"Why does she want you to do that?"

"She says we're too young to get serious."

"What did you say to that, San?"

"I told her to sod off and that I love you."

"I love your command of English, San, you're

so eloquent."

"It's not funny, Doug, I'm sick of her interfering in my life."

"She just looking out for you, San?"

"Tell you what, San, I'll win her round with a box of Milk Tray chocolates and my charm." And I did, with the chocolates and a couple of my jokes (the ones San thinks are crap).

The next day, San came to me and gave me a kiss and said,

"How do you do it?"

"Do what, San?" I said with a grin.

"Be such a bloody charmer."

"It's a gift babe."

"I think that's why I fell for you, Doug."

"But of course, mind you them chocolates cost me a few bob."

"You never change, Doug, you're tight as a duck's..."

"Now, now, San, mind your language, sweetheart."

Then she laughed and put her arm around me and gave me a kiss.

However, a few weeks later none of us were laughing. Just three words would change our lives, especially mine.

Tony rang me with some bad news.

"The bastard's out."

"Who's out?"

"Ronny's out of prison! And he's not coming to wish you a happy birthday." All the memory came back to me of my encounter with Ronny's brother.

I now knew that my life was in danger and San's, too. I would have to make some decisions on what I should do next.

I tell San I think we should end our relationship.

"Who told you Ronny's out?" I asked Tony.

"Raz said that Betty found out from one of her friends."

"Did Razzar say where Ronny is now?"

"No one seems to know where he is."

"Maybe Ronny scared, he's got a lot of people who hate his guts."

"Ronny doesn't scare that easily, and he still has a lot of friends who are just as nasty as him. Raz heard on the grapevine that Ronny may have gone up north to see his brother."

"Another nutter, I suppose."

"Razzar said that Ronny's brother is involved in drugs and is a pusher, that is to say, he sells drugs."

I rolled my eyes and then said, "I know what a pusher is, Tony, I'm from the back streets like you."

"Ronny's brother is just as dangerous as Ronny. He was once accused of attempted murder but got off because no one would testify against him."

"What about the rest of Ronny's gang?"

"They have gone their separate ways, but if Ronny comes back, who knows?"

"Did Raz say anything else?"

"Yes, watch your back!"

"Thanks, Tony, and you do the same."

Later that day I met San in her house while her mam was out. Normally I would have been so happy to be with her, but now I had to say to her that we would have to end our relationship.

"Sit down, San, I need to tell you something."

"Why? what's up?"

I looked at her trying to find the right words and thought I needed to be direct and not mess her around.

"It's about us."

"You're scaring me now, Doug, what is it?"

"I think your mam might have a point, perhaps we are too young to get serious."

"Is there someone else?" San's eyes were beginning to fill up.

I put my hand on her face and then touched her beautiful auburn hair.

"No, there's nobody else. I just think it's the right thing to do. We are young, and we have our whole life in front of us."

"But I want to spend the rest of my life with you, Doug, I thought you wanted to do the same. Please be honest with me and don't give me any crap. Don't...don't you love me anymore?"

"Yes, of course I do."

"Then why are you doing this to me?" The tears were now running down her cheeks.

"Ok San, I'm scared you might get hurt."

"What do you mean by that? Scared of what?"

I then told San everything that Tony had told me and how worried I was that something might happen to her.

"But Ronny might not come back."

"San, do you seriously believe that? You know as well as I do he's got unfinished business here, and he's not going to lose face or his notorious reputation by not coming back."

"Listen, Doug, I think your overreacting here. Why would he come back looking for you over a few words you said to him in the park?"

"But it's not just that, San, there is something I didn't tell you that happened the day after our encounter with them lads in Queens Gardens."

San now started to look really concerned and wanted answers.

"Well, that lad who thought he was a hard case, I met him the following day near where I live, and I lost my temper and hit him."

"Why didn't you just walk away?"

"I couldn't do that, he made comments about you and I saw red and hit him. But I'm afraid it gets worse."

"What do you mean worse?"

"Do you remember what he said that night when he went away?"

"He said, 'you don't know who I am do you?'"

"Yes, it turns out that it was Ronny's younger brother."

San put her hands over her face in horror and then said,

"You bloody idiot!! You're just like your dad, think with your fists and not your head."

"I just couldn't walk away, San."

"Now what do we do, Doug?"

"What do you mean, San, by saying we?"

"Well, I'm going nowhere now, and don't worry, I can look after myself too, so where do we go from here?"

I put my hand on my chin and said, "We just wait for Razzar to come up with something, I suppose."

Where is Ronny now?!

No one heard anything about Ronny for a few weeks, and we were beginning to wonder if he would come back.

But we were getting a bit complacent thinking he might never come back. Razzar was not so sure and said, "Don't think you've heard the last of him yet, he will come back, wait and see."

Then out of the blue Betty said one of her friends on The Orchard Park Estate had heard that he'd been seen in a car going past The Rampant Horse pub on her road.

Razzar then went to The Orchard Park Estate to ask her friend if she had any idea where he might have gone. She told Razzar one of her mates had told her that she was told he'd gone back up north again. "Where does your friend live?"

"It's no good, Raz, going to see her, she's too terrified to say anymore."

Raz then went back to the pub and called a meeting between us all. When I got to the Botanic there was only me, Raz and Betty there.

Razzar told me there was a pint behind the bar for me so

I went to the bar to collect it and sat down between Raz and Betty, "Where's Tony?"

"He told me he can't get away from work, he said they have a big order to get out."

"What do you think Ronny's up to, Raz?"

"Well, he's not helping the aged, I can tell you that, I think he's been dealing drugs with his brother."

"What makes you think he's dealing drugs with his brother?"

"Well, he didn't go to Newcastle for a holiday, Doug...there is something else, too."

Suddenly, I felt a chill up my spine.

"What's that, Raz?"

"It's possible that his brother might pay us a visit too."

"Why do you think that?"

"He might want to expand his little drugs empire with Ronny as his main pusher."

"Well if it's drugs, perhaps Ronny will leave us alone."

"You're bloody optimistic, aren't you, Doug? Don't forget you beat up his younger brother."

"I'm not likely to forget that, Raz, San keeps reminding me."

"Well, I'm telling you, Doug, that Ronny looks after his own and he never forgets those who have upset him."

"Have you warned Tony?"

"Tony's becoming too complacent and that's dangerous, it means you become careless."

"Well what do we do now, Raz?"

"You two keep your head down and tell Tony to do the same and leave the thinking to me."

"And make sure you tell San and tell her to be careful, Doug," said Betty.

"Don't worry, Betty, I'll tell her and take care of her."

"She's a lovely girl and she cares about you so make sure you keep her safe."

"Don't worry, Betty, she means the world to me. I'll make sure she's safe."

I then got the bus to San's house, but now I was really worried about San's safety.

You can't fool everyone all the time.

With all the events taking place of the last few weeks, I decided to keep everything to myself, not letting anyone of the family know what was going off. But I couldn't fool everyone.

One day while I was alone thinking what was going to happen next, my dad came to me. "What's going on, son? What's troubling you?"

Trying hard to hide my own fear and concerns I turned to walk out of the front door. "It's nothing I can't handle, dad, it's nothing for you to worry about."

My dad's words took on a softer tone, "I'm your dad. I'm here if you need me, son, and there will come a time when you will need my help."

"Thanks, dad, I appreciate that, but I need to catch the bus now." I then walked out of the door...

The last thing I wanted was to make things worse by involving my family.

The bus stopped just a short distance from San's house.

It was such a beautiful day, a beautiful blue sky, warm sunshine and just a gentle breeze. I looked around at people walking about without a care in the world, yet I had so many. I had San on my mind all the time. What if she got hurt?

Or I lost her? I wouldn't want to carry on...

I pushed all these things out of my mind as I knocked on her door.

The door opened, and I was greeted by her warm and beautiful smile and a kiss (and I felt so guilty for involving her in all of this).

"Where's your mam?"

"She's gone shopping."

"Oh 'as she?" And I put my arm around her slim waist and looked into her lovely blue eyes.

She smiled and put her arms around my neck and gave me a kiss.

Then she looked at me suspiciously and made it clear that

this was not an invitation to take advantage of the situation.

"Don't get any ideas, Doug."

"You're such an old-fashioned girl, San, and this is not the fifties, it's 1967."

"When the time is right, you will know. Then it will be special for us both." Then she gave me another smile. "When I've got a ring on my finger."

"I will never stop trying, San," I said with a grin.

"Listen, Doug, I've got some good news for you."

"You mean you've changed your mind."

"No, Doug, I haven't changed my mind, but it's still good news."

"Ok San, what's this good news you've got for me?"

"We've got a phone now, Doug, so you can ring me anytime you need me."

"You've got a phone?! How can you afford to have a phone?"

"Them words sound familiar, I asked you that same question a few weeks ago. My mam won some money on

Bingo, so you can ring me now." San quickly wrote the number down on a piece of paper and gave it to me, carefully folded. Then she playfully pointed her finger at me and said, "So now there is no now reason why you can't phone me, ok?"

I slipped the piece of paper into my pocket.

"Ok San, sorry to spoil the mood, but let's talk about something more serious."

San's face dropped, and her expression betrayed her own concerns and worries.

"Ronny."

"Yes, Ronny."

"Have you heard anything?"

"Nothing definite, only that Razzar has been

to have a few words with some ex members of Ronny's Gang."

"He asked them in his usual way."

"You mean he's told them if they don't spill their guts they will be eating hospital food," said San with a smile.

"Well, you know how subtle Raz can be, don't you? I'm pleased he's on our side."

I spent an hour with San and then I remembered Razzar had asked me to meet him again at The Botanic. So I said my goodbyes and said I'd be back as soon as I could.

The Botanic's landlord had changed now so I had a chance of getting a decent pint.

San give me a hug and a kiss, "Take care, or I'll never get my ring and we won't have that special time together."

"Don't worry, San, I'll be careful." Then she watched as I walked to the bus stop.

Good news and bad news

After a short walk to the bus stop, I waited a few minutes for the bus to arrive, and it arrived on time as it always did. I sat down, and the bus conductor came and took my money. Then I looked out of the window and went into a dream-like state.

I hadn't told San that I sold my old clapped-out scooter to an enthusiastic buyer who had a lot more money than me.

I had used that money to buy San the ring she so desperately wanted. I would give it to her in a couple of weeks on her birthday as a surprise.

The bus arrived on Spring Bank not far from the Botanic pub. It was just a few yards' walk to the pub and as I walked into Botanic, Raz and Betty were just finishing their pints. I sat down between Raz and Betty, then Razzar turned to Betty and said, "Go and get three pints for us, babe."

As Betty was collecting our drinks, I asked Raz, "Any news, Raz, about Ronny?"

"Well, I've made some inquiries from one of the ex members of his gang."

"Was that after you let go of his throat?"

"I don't know what you are on about, Doug, I was just adjusting his tie, it wasn't tight enough." He then gave me a grin.

Just then, Betty came back with the beers and sat down next to Razzar. Raz carried on talking. "I've got some good news and some bad news. What do you want to hear first?" I gave a sigh, "I'll have the good news first."

"Well, the good news is Ronny's brother been collared by the police. He was caught selling drugs in Newcastle, and he didn't go quietly, he laid out two coppers, but he got what he deserved when they got him in the police van."

"That's great news, that means that bastard is out of the way now."

"I shouldn't get too excited, Doug, Razzar hasn't told you the bad news yet."

"What's that?"

"Ronny still uncaged, and that animal is just as dangerous, and the police have got nothing on him."

"So where is he?"

"No one knows, and if they do, they too scared to say anything," said Betty.

"Betty's right, no one wants to risk having their heads kicked in, but I have heard his gang are getting more cocky, so my guess is he's around somewhere."

"Where's Tony?"

"He's told me he's working overtime until 9 o'clock tonight."

"Have you told him about all of this?"

Razzar looked concerned and it was reflected in his reply.

"I'm worried about Tony, he doesn't seem to be taking things seriously. If he isn't careful, he could end up getting hurt."

"Why, what did he say?"

"He said he's not worried now that Ronny's brother been arrested, he said Ronny won't do anything now. He'd be too scared, so I told him Ronny doesn't scare that easily and he should be careful, but he doesn't seem that bothered."

"There's not much more you can do, Razzar, let's hope he thinks over what you said."

"I really hope so, Doug."

After we'd been talking for about an hour I looked down at my watch. "I must get off now, I need to tell San about all of this."

Betty replied, "You really are smitten, aren't you, Doug?"

I then made my way back to San's.

Tony pays the price.

The engineering place where Tony worked was situated by the river. To get to it you had to walk down a narrow, cobbled street.

It was only a small firm and employed just ten people, including apprentices like himself.

It was 9 o'clock and he'd just clocked off and said to his workmates, "I'll see you tomorrow, lads."

Then he started walking down the narrow, cobbled street feeling pleased with himself that he'd earned a few more quid towards his new coat. The old town where the engineering factory was at that time wasn't well lit. Tony called the street where the factory was "Ripper Street" and that's just what it looked like.

It was now twilight and the buildings cast eerie shadows along the road. Tony started to feel uneasy like he was being watched. He thought to himself, what's a matter with me? I'm getting paranoid, and then carried on walking.

After going a few yards, he thought he'd heard footsteps behind him. He turned around but saw nothing. He carried a few more steps, then he heard footsteps again, only this time he wasn't imagining it. He looked behind him and he saw two figures in the shadows running towards him with something in their hands. He started running but it was clear they were gaining on him. His hart was beating, and he thought it was coming through his chest and he was panting, trying hard to catch his breath. Sweat was running down his face. He desperately wanted to reach the main road where someone might see him and call for help. As he got to the end of the cobbled road, someone was waiting for him—it was Ronny.

He was trapped like a rabbit in a snare, helpless, waiting for the inevitable.

It wasn't long before Ronny's mates were behind Tony with baseball bats in their hands. Ronny went up to Tony's face and with a twisted smile said, "Tell your mates Ronny's back." At this point, Tony wet himself, then Ronny turned to his mates and said, "Ok, lads, do a good job." Then they started hitting him with their baseball bats while Ronny laughed. When they'd finished, Ronny knelt down beside him, "No one messes with me, tell your mate he's next." Then Ronny spat in his face and ran off.

One of Tony's mates who just happened to be coming down the same road just as Ronny was running off ran to Tony and shouted to someone nearby, "Call for an ambulance!"

Back at San's house

It wasn't a very romantic evening with San's mam there, it was about as comfortable as a pair of tight underpants. It was such a relief when she left the room. I suppose she was just being protective of her daughter. Me and her mam did have a nice chat, though, and I think she now accepted that I was the only one for her daughter.

It was now time to leave and I got up and said goodbye to her mam, then me and San walked to her front door. On the step of her front door, she looked into my eyes and gave me a goodbye kiss that sent my pulse racing, and, so her mam couldn't hear, she whispered in my ear very seductively, "My mam won't always be here, you know."

"Are you saying..."

"Keep your voice down, Doug, mam might hear you."

"I can't wait to see you again, San."

"Doug, when will you say them three words?" I gave her a warm smile and kissed her tenderly. "I don't need to say them words, you already know how I feel."

"San, remember what I told you about what Razzar told me? So be careful what you say to anyone."

"Don't worry, I will. Just make sure you take care of yourself too."

As I walked to the bus stop I knew we were now at last starting to move into a more intimate part of our relationship. I went to the bus intoxicated with my feelings and emotions for her, but why couldn't I bring myself to say them three words? She knew I loved her. I was just frightened of leaving myself vulnerable, but why I don't know. Maybe it's because I never ever heard my dad say that to my mam.

The bus got me home for 11 o'clock and I went straight to bed.

I got up at 8 o'clock and went down to the kitchen and had a strip down wash and was just about to have something to eat when mam called me to the phone. "It's Betty." She

handed me the phone, "Hi, Betty, is everything alright?"

"Razzar's told me to tell you that you have to get down to the infirmary straight away."

"What's a matter, Betty?"

"It's Tony, he's in a bad way."

"Why? Has he had an accident?"

"Razzar said he'll explain when you get there, he said his brother will pick you up."

"Ok, Betty, I'll get dressed straight away." I then put the phone down.

"What's happened, Doug? Is everything ok?"

"It's Tony, mam, he's in hospital, something's happened to him. I've got to get dressed."

I got dressed as quickly as I could just in time to be picked up by Razzar's brother. Five minutes later there was a loud knock on the door.

My dad came down the stairs. "Who the hell is that at the door?"

"It's Razzar's brother, dad, he's taking me to the infirmary, Tony's been hurt, I need to get off. Please ring San and tell her what's happened, tell her I'll give her a ring as soon as I know any more."

I then went out and got into Andy's car and we went straight to the hospital.

Andy was nothing like his brother. He was quite handsome, slim and well-spoken. He certainly wasn't a hard case like his brother. In fact, I doubt if he'd ever been in a fight.

It only took us five minutes to get to the infirmary and we went straight to the reception. We asked where they had taken Tony and told the receptionist that we were family. It was the only way she was going to tell us. She told us he'd been taken to surgery and there was a waiting room nearby.

We went to the waiting room and saw Razzar and Betty there, both looking very anxious and worried. Tony's mam and dad were talking to the doctor.

"What's happened, Raz? Has Tony had an accident?!"

Razzar looked at me with rage and anger on his face, "No, it's that bastard, Ronny."

"Ronny? Are you sure?!"

"Yes, I'm sure, and the doctor 'as just told his mam and dad that Tony might not make it."

I felt sick and highly emotional when Razzar said this. I couldn't bear it if we lost Tony like we lost Pete. Me and Tony had grown up in the same street and played together since we were little kids .

"Are you saying Tony might die?"

"I don't want to think about that, Doug, let's just hope everything will be ok."

Razzar then turned to me and said, "Ronny's made a big mistake because now it's become personal."

"Who found him?" Raz asked Andy.

"One of his workmates apparently."

"Have the police been informed?" I asked.

"It was too dark for Tony's friend to give a description of who did it."

"Then how do you know it was Ronny?"

"I know it's him, I just know. My gut instinct tells me."

"So what now, Raz?"

"Now it's time for us to sort this out ourselves," said Razzar with a menacing look as his eyes narrowed. Then he looked straight at me and said with a snarl, "Now it's payback time."

"But Raz, we have no idea where he is!"

It was then that Betty surprised us all, "I think I might know where you can find him."

We both turned to Betty, both surprised and shocked at her reply.

"Where?!" we both shouted.

"I've rang Sharon up."

"Who the hell is Sharon?" Raz said in amazement.

"She was once a member of Ronny's gang a year ago, but now won't have anything to do with them because of the way they treated her."

"Why didn't she say anything before? And why haven't you mentioned her before?"

"Raz, it would take too long to explain and you're running out of time."

"Do you trust this Sharon?"

"Yes, I do."

"Ok, where is the bastard?"

"Sharon can't be certain, but she's heard that he's stopping with his mate Ryan at 16 Whitewood Close on the Longwood Estate."

Razzar turned to his brother Andy, "Do you know how to get to this place?"

"Yes."

"Then let's go."

So me and Razzar got in Andy's car.

"Put your foot down, Andy."

"Ok, Raz, but I hope there's no coppers around. I don't want a fine."

It only took us ten minutes to reach our destination. The Longwood Estate was a right crap hole, litter everywhere, gardens overgrown with weeds, broken-down fridges and urine-stained mattresses. Me and Raz got out of the car just as Andy was going to follow. Razzar pointed to Andy and in a stern voice said, "You stay there, me and Doug will sort this out."

So we walked down Whitewood Close, curtains twitching all along the road from noisy neighbours. And kids with mucky faces giving us abuse as they ran to their mams and dads. We found number 16 and Razzar went up to the door and hammered it with his big fist. When there was no answer, Razzar lost patience and kicked it with his boot. "Answer this bloody door or I'll kick it in."

Within a couple of minutes, a lanky spotty-faced lad with hair that looked like it hadn't been washed in weeks came to the door. "What the hell do you two want?!"

"Where is he?"

"Who?"

Razzar then grabbed him by the throat and lifted him off the floor. "Is your name Ryan?"

"Yes, what do you want? You're choking me."

"Where is Ronny?"

"I don't know, he just pissed off this morning."

"Where?!"

"How the hell would I know? I'm not his bloody keeper."

Razzar tightened his grip, if I hadn't stopped

him, Raz would have killed him.

Razzar let him go, he obviously didn't know where Ronny was. "I think he would have told you by now to save his own skin." Razzar slowly released his iron-like grip and let him fall to the ground.

Holding his throat, he slowly got up on his feet and said, "You crazy bastard, you could have killed me."

"If I find out you have lied to me I'll be back."

He then punched Ryan in the stomach. "If you see Ronny, tell him Razzar wants a word with him."

We both made our way back to the car.

"Well, Raz, where do we go from here?"

"I'll have another word with Betty, perhaps she's got some more information for me, but mark my words, I'll have Ronny one way or the other. Andy, take us back to the infirmary."

On arriving back to the hospital, we found out that only Tony's family were allowed to see him so we all agreed to go back to the Botanic.

On the way, Betty told us that Tony had undergone emergency surgery because he had a bleed on the back of his brain. Betty had tried to comfort his parents and his brother the best she could. She said that Tony's brother would let us know of any more developments.

I asked Razzar's brother if he wouldn't mind if he dropped me off at San's house and giving me a ring at San's if they found out more important information about Tony. "Ok, Doug, no problem."

San had already been informed of what had gone off and was waiting for me at her house.

Who's Sharon?!

When they got back to the pub Betty went up to the bar to get three pints and brought them to the table where Razzar and Andy were sitting.

"Ok, Betty, tell me about Sharon," said Razzar.
"Sharon and me went to the same school," said Betty.

"What was she like at school?"

"She was always in trouble, but then again, we all were."

"What sort of trouble?"

"Well, from what I can remember, she was always fighting or going off to have a fag behind the bike sheds. She also seemed to like the bad lads. We became good friends and watched each other's backs. I used to tell her, 'why do you always go after the wasters? Why don't you find a decent lad?' But she couldn't help herself. That's how she became involved with Ronny's gang.

"She was besotted with this lad called Dave, he was a right nasty bit of work, a real nutter. He was insanely jealous, she had to be careful who she talked to or looked at. He would burn her with cigarettes every time she upset him. In the end, she left him."

"I'm surprised he let her go that easily, didn't he try to get her back?"

"Yes, Raz, many times he would stalk her or plead to her to go back to him."

"But she said, never would she go back to him again."

"Can you trust her?"

"Yes, I do, Raz."

"Ok, Betty, I'll take your word for it, but for some reason I feel uneasy about her."

"I think you're being a bit paranoid now, Razzar," said Betty.

San and Doug are in danger!

When I went through San's door I smelt her beautiful perfume. It filled the room. And to my surprise and delight, her mam was out. I put my arms around her slim waist and pulled her close to me and gave her a passionate kiss.

We then sat down on her settee and I told her all the things that had gone off that day. She was shocked and upset and she said Tony was in her prayers. She then told me off for taking risks.

I told her about Sharon. San then said, "My mam's friend's daughter is called Sharon. Apparently, she was out of control when she was a kid and went out with some dodgy lads."

"Did you ever meet her?"

"No, but I think she went to Betty's school."

"She must be the same girl then."

"Maybe she is."

"Anyway, Betty seems to trust her, so she must have changed her rebellious ways."

"San then gave me a kiss and said, "Doug I've something to say to you."

"Oh, before you do, I've got something for you."

Then just as I was going to reach in my pocket, to my frustration and annoyance, the phone rang.

"I wonder who that could be?" San picked up the phone and after talking for about a minute she passed the phone on to me.

"Who is it, San?"

"It's a girl, she says she needs to speak to you urgently."

I took the phone off San and asked who it was who was speaking. To my surprise and amazement, it was Sharon.

"I've an urgent message from Betty and Raz for you and San to go to The Rampant Horse. They waiting for you both. It's about Ronny."

"Ok, thanks, Sharon. I'm on my way," and I put the phone down.

"What is it, Doug?"

"It's that girl who knows Betty."

"The girl who we were talking about, Sharon?"

"Yes, apparently Raz and Betty are going to meet us at The Rampant Horse."

"Why there?"

"Me and the lads used to go there a few months ago before we got kicked out for being underage. Why there. I don't know. Razzar must have his reasons, I suppose."

"Let's go, Doug. I'll go and get my coat."

"I think it might be better if you stay here, San."

"Don't be daft, Doug, you trust Sharon, don't you?"

"Yes, if Betty says she trusts her, then I do too."

"Come on, let's go."

So we made our way to the Rampant Horse on The Orchard Park Estate.

As we walked down together, San said that when her mam and dad were together, they used to love that pub.

Meanwhile, Raz and Betty were still talking when the landlord called Betty over and said some girl wanted to talk to her. "Whoever she is, Betty, she's in a bit of a state." Betty quickly went over to the bar and took the phone of the landlord. “Hello? Who is it?”

“It’s Sharon, I’ve done something terrible... I’m sorry. I didn’t mean to do it, he made me do it.”

“Sharon, you’re not making any sense, slow down and tell me what you’ve done.”

“Dave told me to say to Doug and San that you and Raz want to see them urgently at the Rampant Horse on The Orchard Park Estate, but they are walking into a trap, Ronny’s waiting for them.”

“How long ago did you tell them !”

“Five minutes ago.”

“You bloody bitch I trusted you.” Then Betty slammed the phone down.

“Raz we have to go to the Rampant Horse straight away.”

“Why? What’s happened?”

“Sharon just told me that Doug and San are in danger.”

“What the hell are you on about, Betty?”

“Razzar, your gut instinct was right. Sharon betrayed us, we haven’t got time to hang around here.”

Razzar turned to Andy, “Come on, Andy we have to go.” “Where to Raz “

"The Rampant Horse on The Orchard Park Estate."

They all ran to the car which was parked across the road.

"Andy, is my baseball bat in the boot of your car?"

"Yes, why? Are you expecting trouble?"

"Yes, Andy, big trouble, but I want you to pick up Doug's dad first. We're going to need him."

It didn't take long for me and San to get to the Rampant Horse. It was only a few minutes away. We walked in through the front door expecting to see Razzar and Betty waiting for us. They were no way to be seen. My heart started to beat faster. Where were Raz and Betty? Sharon had led us into a trap.

"Where are Razzar and Betty, Doug?"

"San we have to get out of here quickly, we've been led into a trap."

"Doug, I'm scared, really scared."

"Take my hand, San, and follow me."

We ran through the back door into the car park. It was empty except for a couple of parked cars. I breathed a sigh of relief. It looked like we were going to get away safe after all. But I was suddenly grabbed from behind by Ryan, and I couldn't move my arms. Some of Ronny's mates grabbed San too. We were both trapped. Then

Ronny came round the side of the pub with his evil twisted smile.

"Well, well, look who we have here, the tough guy who beat up my brother."

"Let her go, Ronny, she's got nothing to do with all of this." Ronny laughed, "I'll do what I want, Doug, and she can watch me do it."

"Leave him alone, you evil bastard."San shouted.

"Do you want me to shut her up?" shouted one of the girls holding her by the hair.

"No, leave her, I'll sort her out later."

"If you hurt her, I'll kill you, Ronny."

"Your girl's got a lot of spirit, I'll give her that, but now I'm getting bored. It's time I paid you back for what you did to my brother."

"He got what he deserved. I even gave him a chance to walk away, but he didn't listen. Doesn't she deserve that chance too?"

His mate Dave came forward, "Let me have him, Ronny."

"Thanks for the offer, Dave, but this bastard is mine." He then reached into his pocket and pulled out a knife. As Ronny moved towards me, San broke free and ran over to Ronny and jumped onto his back and started to become a wildcat scratching his face and pulling his hair. "You bloody bitch" He pulled her off and then stabbed her in the stomach.

I shouted out, "I'll kill you, Ronny, you evil bastard!" I then dropped my head to my chest and then brought it back with such a force it broke Ryan's nose. I then ran at Ronny in a rage. He caught me on my arm with his knife, but I didn't even notice the blood pouring out. At that point Razzar hit Ronny from behind with his baseball bat. Ronny turned around, but Razzar brought the bat down on Ronny's knife arm shattering his wrist. He then kicked him in the groin. Ronny then fell to the ground.

At the same time, my dad sorted out Dave, catching him on the jaw with his right hook, a blow that resulted in him breaking his jaw. He then caught Ryan as he was legging it out of the car park and with another blow sent Ryan crashing to the ground. Betty shorted out the girls.

While all this was happening, I was beside San desperately trying to stop the bleeding, holding my hand tightly against her wound, but her blood was just oozing through my fingers. She looked at me, tears in her eyes, and said to me, "Say them three words, Doug."

"I love you, San. I always have, and I always will." I then reached in my pocket and took out the ring and put it on her finger. She looked at me with her beautiful blue eyes and said, "I love you too," and then she closed her eyes and died.

It only took a few minutes for the police and the ambulance to arrive. Ronny and his gang were arrested, Raz turned to one of the police officers and said, "Where the hell were you lot when we needed you?"

"I'm so sorry, we got here as soon as we could, but we were held up by a road accident. I'm sorry to ask you at this time but all of you have to come with us to the Station."

The medical team said to me, "You need to let her go now, son, there's nothing more you can do." But I wouldn't let her go. I looked at my dad, unable to see clearly because of my tears, and said, "She's gone, dad." My dad replied, "I know, son, but we need to get you to the hospital."

While I was at the hospital being stitched up, I was experiencing such pain my heart was hurting so much. As the nurse was stitching my arm, I looked on in bewilderment and asked, "Why?" I kept replaying the event over and over again. I let San down, it was all my fault, it should have been me. I just wanted to die.

After I was seen by the doctor, I too gave a statement of all the events that took place in the car park of The Rampant Horse.

We all gave statements at the police station and all my clothes were taken and examined by the police and kept for evidence.

Although they all came to me to try and comfort me, no words could take away the pain I was feeling. Betty came to me and put her arm around me and said, "Just let the tears come, don't try to hold them back, Doug. It's all part of the grief you have to go through."

Razzar and my dad didn't know what to say, what could they say? San was dead.

"How is San's mam and dad?"

"I'm sure you know the answer to that, Doug, they are in a lot of pain too, just like you," said my dad.

"I can't believe I've just asked that question, I'm sorry, I'm not thinking straight. Dad, it's my fault, I should have known it was a trap."

"It's not your fault, son, you didn't know, you were doing what you thought was right at the time."

Tears filled my eyes again, "I told San that I would look after her and now she's dead." I suddenly felt I was going to be sick, so I asked the police officer where the toilet was and ran to it. I then vomited into it, then I fell to my knees and just sobbed and sobbed.

Shortly afterwards, my dad came in, "The police have just said we can take you home now, son. I've brought you some clean clothes." So I got dressed and followed my dad out.

It had been three long hours of continuous questions and I was racked with guilt. Andy took me and my dad home, all along the way I kept having flashbacks of the events that took place in that car park. I kept seeing San's face and the tears running down her cheeks and her last words to me. The words that would haunt me for the rest of my life.

When I got home, my mam put her arm around me, "I'm so sorry, Doug." My dad asked my mam to get me something to eat. "I'm alright, mam, I'm not hungry, I just want to be left alone." I then went upstairs and closed the door.

At the chapel of rest

Two days later I went to see San at the chapel of rest with Razzar and Betty. She looked so beautiful, as if she was in a deep sleep. I then touched her auburn hair and it brought back all the memories we had together. Our times in Peason's Park where we first met and Queens Gardens and other places, we were so happy. I then bent over and kissed her goodbye.

On the way out, we met San's mam and dad.

San's dad walked over to me with anger and rage on his face. If Razzar hadn't stepped between us, I would have paid the price of his malice. Then San's mam turned to me as she was going into the chapel of rest and spat out her venom, "I hate you, I despise you, if she hadn't met you she would still be alive today." She then looked at me with contempt and then went into the chapel of rest in floods of tears.

It would be five years before San's mam forgave me for the death of her daughter.

Razzar said, "let's get you home."

Andy drove me home and then I went straight upstairs and closed the bedroom door. My mam came up and knocked on the door, "Doug, are you alright?"

"Yes, mam, I just need to be left alone for a while."

"Can I get you something to eat or drink?" My mam was trying to do what she thought was best.

"No, mam, I'm alright." I then put my head in my hands and thought to myself, San's mam was right, if she hadn't met me, she would still be alive.

I wouldn't leave my room for days but was full of self-loathing. I should never have taken her to the Rampant Horse that night, I should never have believed that lying bitch.

San's funeral.

San's funeral was held on the 15th of September at 3:30 at Our Lady of Mercy. It was attended by all her friends and family. Sally was there too, with her arm around San's mam offering her comfort in her time of grief.

But me and Betty with Raz sat at the back of the church to avoid any confrontation with her mam and dad. It was a lovely day for San, the sun was shining. But as they brought her coffin out, it started to rain as if it was raining tears.

I couldn't take anymore so I asked Razzar to take me home.

For six weeks I wouldn't eat properly. I didn't even wash. I just wanted to be by myself. My mam and dad tried their best to lift my spirits, but it made no difference. And then one day my younger sister Maggie came in my room while I was crying and said, "I don't want you to cry anymore so I bought you this flower to give it to you from the garden." I looked at her hand, it wasn't a flower, just a daisy, but she didn't know it was only a weed. I gave her a hug.

I was so touched by this act of kindness, she was only six. I now realized I couldn't go on like this, so I took her little hand and led her downstairs. I then went and had a wash and washed my hair. I put some clean clothes on and had something to eat. My mam and dad were amazed but so relieved.

"Mam, there is something I have to do."

"What's that, Doug?"

"I have to say one last goodbye."

"Are you going to the cemetery?"

"No, mam, but it is a special place."

"Why? What do you mean?"

My dad put his arm around my mam and said, "Let the lad go."

I then went out of my house and walked to the bottom of our street and then walked down the ten-foot and made my way to Peason's Park. I then went to the cow shed and sat down. "Well, San, this is where we met, and this is where I say my last goodbye. I will always love you." I stayed there for over an hour with tears running down my cheeks then I got up and left the cow shed and made my way home.

The trial

Ronny had been remanded in custody for six months before his trial.

The trial took place on the 28th of March at Hull crown court. After weeks of grieving, my emotions had now turned to hate. I now had to get my head together and focus on giving evidence with my Dad, Razzar, Betty and Andy. Nothing focuses your mind so much as hate.

As me and my dad were getting ready, my dad turned to me and said, "The bastard will get what's coming now, son."

"Yes dad, but it won't be the rope, will it?" As soon as we had finished getting ready, Andy arrived to take us to the crown court. We all remained silent as Andy drove us to the court, we all had our memories of that dreadful night to deal with. We had to make sure we got all the details right.

The court case went on for three weeks and we were all cross examined by his barrister over and over again. We all had to listen to all the crap about his childhood and how he was treated by his dad.

All I wanted was to see justice and to see Ronny go down. I didn't care how clever his barrister was at defending him. He had taken San from me, the most precious thing that had meant the world to me. Casandra, or San as I always called her. San had always said to me, "Don't ever call me Casandra, it's too pretentious, just call me San."

The day came for the court to give its verdict and we all knew what the answer was going to be.

The judge asked the defendant to rise and said,

"This court finds Ronny W...guilty of the manslaughter of Cassandra M...And passes the sentence of fifteen years' imprisonment." San's mam and dad shouted out, "Hang the bastard, hang the bastard." As Ronny was being led away by the court attendants, he looked up at me and gave me his twisted smile. It took the combined strength of my dad and Raz to hold me back.

Ryan and Dave got six years for their part in San's death. But me and San's parents got a life sentence. My dad turned to me. "It's over now, son, it's time to look to the future and start living again." And although it was hard to accept what he said, I knew he was right.

Looking forward to the future

Two years have now passed, and many things have changed. I have learned that broken hearts do heal in time, and that hate can destroy us all if we let it...

Razzar and Tony have called for me to go to our local pub. (Tony has long since recovered.) We are all brothers once more; we were always inseparable and still are, after all, brothers stick together, don't they?

Now, although I didn't realize it at the time, my life was going to change forever, and I would be happy again.

Razzar for once had a tie on and was smartly dressed. And Tony looked the business, too, just like he always did.

Raz said, "We think it's time for you to start

living again."

"Yes, you've been a miserable sod too long, it's time for you to revive that charm again, but no more crap jokes, ok?" said Tony.

"What are you two up to?"

"We're all going to the Locarno dance hall like we used too."

"I don't know, Raz, it's been a long time, and I think I've lost what charm I had. I'm not the same lad I was."

"You do talk some crap, Doug, you are still the Doug we've always known, you just need to get on the saddle again."

I was reluctant to go and was just about to say no when something inside me said, Why not? What have you got to lose?

"Ok, you've twisted my arm. I'll come."

"There is just one thing, Doug."

"And what's that, Tony?"

"You buy the first pint."

"But I bought the last one."

"Yes, Doug, but that was two years ago."

"You always was a tight sod, as tight as a ducks..." said Raz.

We all laughed just like we used to, it felt good to be alive again. That night I met my future wife and it was the start of a new story...

I say goodbye to Middleton street.

Well, here I am at the top of our street getting ready to say goodbye.

I have lived here for seventeen years and had so many happy times, and some sad times too. Such sweet and bitter memories, but mostly sweet memories I will take with me.

In a few minutes, Andy will pick me, dad and mam and take me to the Railway station. So I take one last walk to the top of my street and my eyes start to fill up once more. As I look down our street, all my childhood memories come flooding back. Me and Tony playing marbles when we were still little kids. So I dry my eyes and start walking home for the last time. On the way, I pass some girls playing Queenie, singing,

"Queenie, Queenie who's got the ball, is he tall or is he small?" A few yards down the road some other girls are playing Hop Scotch. I smile at them as I make my way to my house. It all takes me back as I'm writing this last chapter.

Now I go through our front door and all my brothers and sisters are waiting to say goodbye. So I give my sisters a hug and a kiss and my brothers a hug. A few minutes later, Andy pulls up outside our house, "Are you ready then?" My dad picks up my suitcase and puts it in the boot of Andy's car. Then Andy gets in his car and drives me and mam and dad to the Station. I look through the window as my brothers and sisters wave me off.

It's only a short drive to the Railway Station, and when we get there, my friends are ready to see me off.

My train is on time and I say my last goodbyes to my mates and they wish me all the best in my new home in Wales.

My mam gives me a kiss and a warm hug, "Take care, Doug, make sure you ring us every week." Trying to hold back the tears, I say back, "I will, mam, I promise, and you make sure you look after yourself too." My dad now gives me a hug and then turns away, so I don't see him cry. I get on the train and the whistle blows and I wave goodbye to everyone.

Epilogue...

I got married on the 17th of March 1973.

Razzar was my best man and Tony was there too. I was later best man for Raz a year later. They had two lovely kids, a boy and a girl like Betty had always wanted.

Tony married a girl called Mary, but sadly she died two years later. However, he later went on to marry again and had a son.

Me and Sue went on to have two kids, a daughter called Beth and a son called Lee, who we love very much.

Although my story was fictional and the events in The Rampant Horse never happened, I have still put a few elements into the story that are true. This mainly concerns my own family and my life at that time. Ronny's gang is also a fictional part of the story. But the book reflects what life was like for many of us in the sixties in Hull.

The End.

A finale note:

Although I have used some swear words in my stories I have tried to limit them as much as possible.

I no longer use the swear words like I used to, so I wanted to limit their use. Also, I don't advocate any type of violence (and I never did, except of necessity when I had no choice).

-Doug Cowie

Me with my brothers in 1969, I'm on the right

Middelton Street. And the top photo, me and my oldest sister the year of the fire in Trinity street.

My mam and dad before they got married

My mam and dad around ten years after I left Hull

Printed in Great Britain
by Amazon

26605653R00096